LIBRARY

LIBRARY

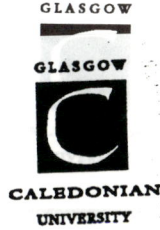

GLASGOW

GLASGOW

C

**CALEDONIAN
UNIVERSITY**

London: H M S O

Researched and written by Reference Services, Central Office of Information.

ISBN 0 11 701729 9

♔HMSO

HMSO publications are available from:

HMSO Publications Centre
(Mail, fax and telephone orders only)
PO Box 276, London SW8 5DT
Telephone orders 071-873 9090
General enquiries 071-873 0011
(queuing system in operation for both numbers)
Fax orders 071-873 8200

HMSO Bookshops
49 High Holborn, London WC1V 6HB   071-873 0011
Fax 071-873 8200 (counter service only)
258 Broad Street, Birmingham B1 2HE   021-643 3740   Fax 021-643 6510
Southey House, 33 Wine Street, Bristol BS1 2BQ
0272 264306   Fax 0272 294515
9-21 Princess Street, Manchester M60 8AS   061-834 7201   Fax 061-833 0634
16 Arthur Street, Belfast BT1 4GD   0232 238451   Fax 0232 235401
71 Lothian Road, Edinburgh EH3 9AZ   031-228 4181   Fax 031-229 2734

HMSO's Accredited Agents
(see Yellow Pages)

and through good booksellers

Contents

Introduction	1
Government Policy and Administration	3
Housing Conditions	7
Owner-occupied Housing	20
Public Rented Housing	28
Housing Associations	44
Private Rented Housing	53
Home Improvement and Rehabilitation	56
Homelessness	67
Future Developments	75
Addresses	79
Further Reading	80
Index	82

Consumers

Acknowledgments

This book has been compiled with the co-operation of several organisations, including other government departments and agencies. The Central Office of Information would like to thank all those who have contributed their comments, and in particular the Department of the Environment, the Department of Health, the Northern Ireland Office, The Scottish Office, the Welsh Office and the Housing Corporation. The assistance of the Civic Trust with the photographs is also appreciated.

Cover photograph credits
Jane Darbyshire Associates (bottom right);
Department of the Environment (bottom left).

Introduction

Housing is a very important part of people's lives. Buying a house is the most important investment that most people in Britain[1] will ever make. Assisting with the provision of housing and relieving homelessness are significant parts of the work of government in Britain, both central and local. The scale of government activity on housing can be gauged from the fact that the Government proposes to spend some £8,400 million on housing in the 1992–93 financial year in England alone, including a £600 million short-term programme to help the housing market, and around £8,000 million in each of the following three years. Total public investment in housing in Scotland is planned to total £900 million in 1992–93. In Northern Ireland, gross 1992-93 expenditure is planned at some £531 million.

Housing conditions in Britain have improved considerably during the twentieth century. Nearly all homes now have the basic amenities such as sanitation and plumbing, and most of the housing stock is in good condition. The total housing stock has grown faster than the number of households, although figures for surpluses of houses conceal local housing shortages, especially in London. However, changing household patterns, including a declining average-household size and a considerable increase in the number of one-person households, has led to changes in the sorts of

---

[1] The term 'Britain' is used informally in this book to mean the United Kingdom of Great Britain and Northern Ireland. 'Great Britain' comprises England, Scotland and Wales.

housing needed. The structure of housing provision has been reformed significantly by recent legislation.

The promotion of home ownership and more choice in the rented sector are key aspects of government housing policy. New house construction is undertaken by both public and private sectors, but the majority of dwellings are built by the private sector for sale to owner-occupiers. Housing associations (see p. 44) are now the main providers of new housing in the subsidised rented sector ('social housing'), although in Northern Ireland the main provider of social housing is the Northern Ireland Housing Executive (see p. 50). Local authorities are being encouraged to see their housing role as more of an enabling one, working with housing associations and the private sector to increase the supply of low-cost housing for rent, without necessarily providing it themselves. In order to stimulate the private rented sector, which has declined to just 8 per cent of the total stock, rents on new private sector lettings were deregulated in 1988 (see p. 54). The Secretary of State for the Environment in England and the Secretaries of State for Wales, Scotland and Northern Ireland are responsible for formulating housing policy and supervising the housing programme. Although the policies are broadly similar throughout Britain, statutory provisions in Northern Ireland and Scotland differ somewhat from those in England and Wales, and administrative arrangements in Wales differ from those in England. Further information on developments in housing is contained in *Current Affairs: A Monthly Survey*, published by HMSO.

Government Policy and Administration

Government Objectives

The Government set out its policy on housing in White Papers published in September and November 1987; the first covering England and Wales and the second relating to Scotland. These set out four main objectives for housing policy:

—the Government would continue to spread home ownership as widely as possible, continuing tax relief on mortgage interest payments (see p. 24) and pressing on with the Right to Buy (see p. 33);

—it would stimulate the independent rented sector and allow housing associations to expand their provision of housing at affordable rents;

—local authority provision of housing should gradually be diminished, while alternative forms of tenure and tenant choice should be developed (see pp. 36–40); and

—the Government would focus the use of public money more effectively while encouraging more businesslike management of the existing stock through a new financial regime for local authorities (see p. 29).

Many of these objectives have since been reflected in legislation. For example, the Housing Act 1988 and the Housing (Scotland) Act 1988 deregulated rents in the private rented sector to encourage investment by new landlords, while the Local Government and Housing Act 1989 introduced a new capital finance system for local authorities, which allows for more effective targeting of public funds.

The Government is committed to further improvements in housing provision and rights, including:

—compulsory competitive tendering of the management of council houses and flats (see p. 40);

—a new right for council tenants to receive compensation for home improvements, and an improved Right to Repair (see p. 30);

—a new nationwide Rents to Mortgages scheme (see p. 36);

—the right for residential leaseholders in blocks of flats to acquire the freehold of the block, and the right for other leaseholders to buy a renewed lease, both at market price (see p. 75); and

—a new 'Rent a Room' scheme to enable homeowners to let rooms to lodgers without paying tax on the rent they receive (see p. 54).

Administration

The Secretary of State for the Environment is responsible for formulating housing policy and supervising the housing programme in England. The Secretaries of State for Wales, for Scotland and for Northern Ireland have similar responsibilities in their respective areas.

Most public housing in Great Britain is provided by 460 local housing authorities. These are:

—in metropolitan areas of England and Wales, the metropolitan districts and London borough councils;

—in non-metropolitan areas of England and Wales, the district councils; and

—in Scotland, the district and islands councils.

The local housing authorities also have important statutory responsibilities towards housing, for example, with regard to homelessness (see p. 68) and the payment of renovation grants (see p. 56), and as landlords. State-assisted housing is also provided by a large number of housing associations under the supervision of the Housing Corporation and its equivalents (see p. 45). In Northern Ireland, housing functions are fulfilled by the Northern Ireland Housing Executive; among its activities it provides social housing directly, assists housing associations, pays home improvement grants and deals with homelessness.

Research

The Government undertakes a large programme of research into housing. The Department of the Environment's 1992–93 housing research programme totals £7.6 million, and new projects are looking at subjects such as energy efficiency in houses, homelessness, empty properties and mortgage repossessions. Other continuing projects include:

—the evaluation of Estate Action schemes (see p. 58) in inner city estates;

—the housing needs of elderly people;

—housing aspects of AIDS/HIV; and

—follow-up work on the 1991 English House Condition Survey.

Planning for Housing

The Government advises local planning authorities to ensure the availability of a five-year supply of housing land, judged against the scale of development provided for in their development plans.[2] These plans should take into account the increasingly varied types of housing requirement, such as those for single people, small households and the elderly.

Irrespective of whether or not an application is on a site identified for housing, each proposal for house-building needs planning permission from the local planning authority. Considerations to be taken into account are likely to include such matters as the overall scale and density of the development, layout and landscaping, and access and parking arrangements. In order to meet the objectives of providing new housing and conserving the countryside, it is important that effective use is made of land within existing urban areas, although it is important to protect urban open spaces. Nearly half the land developed for housing was either previously developed or was vacant land in built-up areas. It is important to ensure that new development in rural areas is sensitively related to the existing pattern of settlement and has proper regard to the protection of the countryside.

[2] For more information about development plans and Britain's system of land-use planning, see *Planning* (Aspects of Britain: HMSO, 1992).

Housing Conditions

Among the important sources of data on housing conditions and the housing stock in Britain are the General Household Survey carried out annually in Great Britain, and the English House Condition Survey and its equivalents. The most recent English House Condition Survey for which data has been published related to 1986; a further survey was carried out in 1991 and it is expected that the results of this will be published in 1993. Statistical information is published in an annual government report, *Housing and Construction Statistics.*

Housing Stock

The housing stock in Britain at the end of 1991 consisted of some 23.6 million dwellings, up 9 per cent from the end of 1981. Of the total, some 19.7 million were situated in England, 1.2 million in Wales, 2.1 million in Scotland and 576,000 in Northern Ireland. Table 1 shows the size of the housing stock in the different parts of Britain over the period 1981–1991.

Table 1: Stock of Dwellings by Country

Thousands at end of year

	England	Wales	Scotland	Northern Ireland
1981	18,021	1,089	1,970	500
1986	18,852	1,128	2,050	535
1991	19,725	1,179	2,142	576

Source: *Housing and Construction Statistics*

There is a crude surplus of dwellings in Britain, in that there are more homes than households (see Table 2 for data on England and Wales). However, this crude surplus does not take into consideration such factors as people owning second homes, a number of 'hidden households' (where people who would wish to move out into their own household cannot for lack of other accommodation), and vacant property. Taking these factors into account, and such trends as an increasing tendency for people to live on their own, there remains a need for more homes (see pp. 68–74 for homelessness and the measures that are being taken to combat it).

Table 2: Households and Dwellings

Thousands

	Number of dwellings end 1991	Number of households mid 1991	Surplus of dwellings
England	19,725	19,036	689
North	1,286	1,210	76
Yorkshire and Humberside	2,025	1,982	43
East Midlands	1,644	1,602	42
East Anglia	875	821	54
Greater London	2,889	2,774	115
Rest of South East	4,356	4,226	130
South West	1,964	1,882	82
West Midlands	2,093	2,045	48
North West	2,594	2,493	101
Wales	1,179	1,095	84

Source: *Housing and Construction Statistics*

The number of properties in Britain is being augmented by housebuilding, in which there was considerable activity during the

1980s. Between 1982 and 1991, 1.8 million dwellings were added to the stock in Great Britain, mostly through new building. Over the same period, 210,000 dwellings were demolished. As the average size of households diminishes, the number of homes is also being increased by the conversion of houses into separate smaller flats; it is estimated that 75,000 extra homes were provided in this way in London alone between 1981 and 1990. Such properties are often suitable as starter homes for young people. Table 3 shows the number of permanent homes completed in Britain in recent years by different types of builder.

Table 3: Number of Dwellings Completed in Britain

	Private sector	Housing assoc- iations	Local author- ities	Other public sector	Total
1981	115,022	19,291	54,867	10,618	199,798
1982	125,398	13,137	33,244	4,033	175,812
1983	148,050	16,136	32,833	2,292	199,311
1984	159,416	16,613	31,699	2,354	210,082
1985	156,507	13,123	26,115	1,102	196,847
1986	170,427	12,521	21,587	1,289	205,824
1987	183,731	12,545	18,823	1,280	216,379
1988	199,331	12,760	19,030	739	231,860
1989	179,536	13,866	16,465	1,164	211,031
1990	156,388	17,077	15,780	931	190,176
1991	148,248	19,498	9,457	625	177,828

Source: *Housing and Construction Statistics*

Age of Property

Although there are many old houses in Britain, over half the housing stock was built after the second world war (1939–45). Table 4 shows the age of the stock in Great Britain. There is some considerable variation in the age of the stock, with, for example, some 21 per cent of the stock in Wales being pre-1891, compared with only 11 per cent of the stock in Scotland. There is also considerable regional variation within England, where 11 per cent of the stock in the West Midlands is pre-1891, compared with over 19 per cent in the South West.

Table 4: Estimated Age-Distribution of Dwelling Stock

Per cent

	Pre-1891	1891–1918	1919–1944	1945–1970	Post-1970
England	14.2	12.2	19.9	31.5	22.2
Wales	20.7	16.5	13.0	29.2	20.6
Scotland	10.6	14.7	16.3	35.4	23.1
Great Britain	14.0	12.6	19.0	32.1	22.3

Source: *Housing and Construction Statistics*

Type of Property

There is a considerable variety of housing types within the stock. Table 5 gives the proportion of households in 1990 occupying different types of property; this shows that over two-thirds of households in Britain live in houses, but that there are a significant number who live in flats. Among those who rent their accommodation from the local authority, the proportion living in flats rises to almost two-fifths, while very few council houses indeed are detached—only 1 per cent of council tenants live in detached

houses. The same is true to an even greater extent of housing association tenants, 60 per cent of whom live in flats.

Table 5: Type of Accommodation Occupied

	Per cent
Detached house	20
Semi-detached house	33
Terraced house	27
Purpose-built flat or maisonette	14
Converted flat or maisonette/rooms	5
With business premises	1

Source: *General Household Survey 1990*

The type of accommodation built varies considerably by age
—a large number of converted flats, for example, are fairly old,
while purpose-built flats tend to be fairly modern. A large proportion of detached houses are of modern construction, while many
terraced houses are older, with nearly two-fifths being built before
1919. Accommodation shared with business premises—such as
shopkeepers living above the shop—also tends to be quite old.
Property built in 1965 or later is fairly evenly divided between
detached, semi-detached and terraced houses and purpose-built
flats, which formed respectively 28, 24, 24 and 22 per cent of the
post-1964 stock.

High-rise flats form a relatively small proportion of the housing stock. In England in 1986 only 16 per cent of flats were in
blocks of six or more storeys, while only 7 per cent were in blocks
of 12 or more storeys. Most of these were in the local authority sector, and the majority were built after 1964. However, the building
of this type of property has virtually ceased in recent years.

Construction Methods

The great majority of houses and flats are of traditional masonry construction—that is, built of bricks or breeze blocks. The English House Condition Survey 1986 identified that there were about 800,000 non-traditional houses in England—built of frame or panel construction in timber, steel or reinforced concrete—and a similar number of non-traditional flats. Over three-fifths of such dwellings belonged to local authorities. The 1986 Welsh House Condition Survey identified 60,000 non-traditional houses, two-thirds of which belonged to local authorities. The emergence of defects in some system-built properties has caused difficulties, especially for those former tenants who had bought from their local authority under the Right to Buy. The Government has therefore introduced measures to deal with these problems (see p. 35).

Temporary Homes

Temporary homes are sometimes erected on vacant plots, mostly using non-traditional methods. A large number of these are still post-war 'prefabs' put up on bomb sites; although designed to be temporary they have generally lasted well. The English House Condition Survey 1986 found that there were some 61,000 temporary dwellings in England, largely in private ownership.

Mobile Homes

An increasing number of people in Britain live in mobile homes. A 1991 survey[3] found that the number of pitches for mobile homes in England and Wales had grown from 59,000 in 1977 to 77,000 in

[3] See **Further Reading**, p. 80.

1991. The 1992 Mobile Homes Survey found that, while mobile home standards can vary considerably, almost 90 per cent of mobile homes surveyed were designed for permanent residential occupation. Many mobile homes look much like normal bungalows.

Sheltered Housing

Sheltered housing, which generally comprises accommodation with an alarm system and warden support, may be provided for elderly people who need support. 'Very sheltered' housing may be provided for the frail elderly, giving in addition a degree of care and enhanced communal facilities. Increasing emphasis is being placed on schemes to help elderly people to continue to live in their own homes; these include home improvement agency services (see p. 61) and adaptations to existing housing to meet the needs of disabled people.

The private sector also provides for the construction of purpose-built retirement homes.

Tenure

The proportion of owner-occupied properties in Britain has been rising strongly during the course of the twentieth century, with the number of privately-rented properties in decline. Renting from local authorities rose strongly in earlier years, but has recently declined, with many council tenants taking advantage of the Right to Buy to buy their homes. The housing association sector remains small but is growing strongly, with the Government seeing it as the main provider of new social housing. Table 6 shows the recent trends in tenure.

Table 6: Tenure in Britain

Per cent, end of year

	1981	1986	1991
Owner-occupied	56.6	62.7	67.7
Rented privately or with a job/business	10.9	8.6	7.4
Rented from housing association	2.2	2.5	3.1
Rented from local authority	30.3	26.2	21.8

Source: *Housing and Construction Statistics*

Owner-occupation is the most common form of tenure for houses; most flats by contrast are rented, largely from local authorities but with a significant number from private landlords (especially in the case of converted flats or 'bedsitter' rooms). Local authority houses tend to be semi-detached or terraced.

Different types of property suit different types of household; for example families are more likely to live in houses, while flats tend to be popular with single adults and young couples. This is connected with the sort of facilities that different types of property offer; houses for example tend to be significantly larger than flats. Table 7 (p. 15) shows data on the sorts of household that live in different types of property.

Regional Variations

Tenure varies considerably by region, as is shown in Table 8. Owner-occupation is highest in the South East outside Greater London, and the South West; it is lowest in Scotland and the north of England. However, in general owner-occupation has been growing faster in those areas where it is currently low—for example, between April 1981 and December 1990, the proportion of

Table 7: Type of Accommodation by Household Type

Per cent

	One adult aged 16-59	Two adults aged 16-59	Small family	Large family
Detached house	9	20	20	20
Semi-detached house	21	33	36	41
Terraced house	25	28	29	32
Purpose-built flat or maisonette	28	12	11	5
Converted flat or maisonette/rooms	16	6	3	2
With business premises/other	1	1	1	0

	Large adult household	Two adults at least one aged 60+	One adult aged 60+
Detached house	27	26	14
Semi-detached house	39	34	26
Terraced house	28	25	23
Purpose-built flat or maisonette	4	11	30
Converted flat or maisonette/rooms	1	3	6
With business premises/other	1	1	1

Source: *General Household Survey 1990*

owner-occupiers in Scotland grew by 15.6 percentage points. By contrast, in the South East, outside Greater London, it rose by only 10.7 percentage points. Housing associations provide over 5 per cent of housing in Greater London, but about 2 per cent in Northern Ireland, the South West and the East Midlands.

Table 8: Tenure by Region, December 1990

Per cent

	Owner-occupied	Private/rented/other	Housing association	Local authority
England	69.1	7.6	3.2	20.1
North	60.8	6.9	3.8	28.5
Yorkshire and Humberside	66.5	7.5	2.2	23.8
East Midlands	70.9	7.9	1.9	19.4
East Anglia	70.5	10.2	2.9	16.3
Greater London	62.1	8.6	5.3	23.9
Rest of South East	74.8	7.8	2.8	14.6
South West	73.9	9.7	1.9	14.5
West Midlands	68.1	5.9	2.8	23.2
North West	68.7	5.7	3.8	21.8
Wales	72.0	6.6	2.5	18.9
Scotland	52.8	5.5	3.3	38.4
Northern Ireland	65.6	3.5	2.0	28.5

Source: *Housing and Construction Statistics*

Income

Tenure is strongly affected by income, with the better-off being overwhelmingly owner-occupiers and those less well-off more likely to be tenants. Some 93 per cent of those households with gross weekly incomes exceeding £600 are owner-occupiers; this figure falls to 26 per cent among those whose incomes are less than £75, the majority of such houses being owned outright rather than on a mortgage. Many of these owner-occupiers are pensioners, whose income is low but who would have a large stock of accumulated wealth in the shape of their home. The Government aims to spread the benefits of owner-occupation, for example, by such means as Rents to Mortgages schemes (see p. 36).

Vacant Property

The English House Condition Survey 1986 found that about 4 per cent of the stock in England was vacant. Of these properties, a large number had only recently become vacant; a significant proportion were for sale or had already been sold and were awaiting re-occupation. The vacancy rate was higher in the private sector than for local authority stock, and over half the vacant dwellings were built before 1919.

Amenities and Repair

The number of dwellings in Britain lacking the basic amenities has been falling steadily for many years. Very few homes are not now fitted with a bath and shower and inside lavatory, while the majority also have central heating. Table 9 shows how the prevalence of these amenities has grown. Virtually all owner-occupied and publicly-rented dwellings have the amenities of bathroom and lavatory; the lack of them is most prevalent in the privately-rented sector.

The English House Condition Survey 1986 showed there to be little change in the state of repair of the stock. Just over a million dwellings were in serious disrepair (that is, with defects costing over £7,000 to rectify), which was about the same number as in 1981.

Table 9: Amenities 1971–90

			Per cent
	1971	1981	1990
Bath or shower			
sole use	88	96	98
shared	3	2	1
none	9	2	1
WC			
sole use	96	98	99
shared	3	2	–
none	1	–	–
Central heating			
night storage heaters only	8	6	8
other central heating only	26	52	72
both kinds	1	–	–
neither kind	65	41	20

Note: -= < 0.5%   Source: *General Household Survey 1990*

In Wales, the level of stock lacking basic amenities was reduced from 8 to 4 per cent between 1981 and 1986. The proportion in serious disrepair was about 1.5 per cent, as opposed to 4.5 per cent in 1981. The number of homes in Wales with roof insulation increased from 60 to almost 79 per cent.

Overcrowding

Very few homes in Britain are now overcrowded. According to the 1989 General Household Survey, only 3 per cent of households were overcrowded according to their 'bedroom standard', a mea-

sure of whether the household had sufficient sleeping accommodation. This marks a considerable reduction in overcrowding since
1971, when 7 per cent of households were overcrowded on this
measure.

The legal definition of overcrowding is given in the Housing
Act 1985 and the Housing (Scotland) Act 1987. These Acts make it
an offence for an occupier to overcrowd a building and for a landlord to permit it to become overcrowded. They also give local
authorities various powers and duties to prevent overcrowding.

Owner-occupied Housing

Owner-occupied housing is now the major form of tenure in Britain. The main form of government assistance to owner-occupiers is through tax relief on mortgage interest payments (see p. 24). Tax is payable on the purchase of houses in the form of stamp duty—this is levied at a rate of 1 per cent on transactions over £30,000. From December 1991 to August 1992 this threshold was temporarily raised to £250,000 as an encouragement to the housing market.

Types of Ownership

Owner-occupied homes are either occupied freehold or leasehold. In the former tenure, which is now usual for houses, the owner owns the property and the land on which it stands outright. In the latter, which is usual for flats, each individual flat is held on a long lease—typically granted for periods of 99 or 125 years—and the leaseholder has to pay a small annual ground rent to the freeholder. In blocks of flats, there will also be a service charge to cover items such as the cost of lighting communal areas and looking after the garden. Leaseholders have certain rights to deal with bad landlords, including the right to apply to the court for the appointment of a manager or the compulsory acquisition of the landlord's interest where there is proof of bad management; the Government is proposing to strengthen these rights. It also intends to give long leaseholders the right to enfranchise and collectively purchase the freehold whether the landlord wishes to sell or not. Most leaseholders in houses already have the right to enfranchise under the Leasehold Reform Act 1967.

House Building

The majority of new homes built in Britain are provided through the private sector. Most new houses are covered by warranty arrangements provided either by the National House-Building Council or the Housing Standards Company Ltd. Both organisations set standards and enforce them by inspection, and provide cover against major structural defects for not less than ten years.

An important constraint on the construction of new homes is the availability of land, which is controlled through the planning system.[4] Proposals for new house-building can often meet strong opposition from local residents. As a result, pressures for land are particularly acute in the heavily-populated South East of England. The Government announced in July 1992 that there would be no increase in the amount of land allocated annually for housing in the South East. One proposed solution to avoiding urban sprawl is the construction of new settlements (see p. 76).

Local authorities are responsible, through their building control sections, to ensure that new houses, and structural alterations to existing ones, conform to the Government's building regulations. These cover matters such as structural integrity, fire safety, noise insulation, hygiene, drainage and ventilation.

House Prices

There have been some considerable fluctuations in the price of houses in recent years. However, since the 1960s house prices have

[4] For further information about Britain's planning system, see *Planning* (Aspects of Britain: HMSO, 1992).

generally risen considerably in real terms, with certain periods of sharp increases, such as 1971–73, 1978–80 and 1986–89. Since 1989, house prices have tended to fall as a result of generally high interest rates, the recession and a depressed housing market. Table 10 shows the average price for houses in Britain in recent years, unadjusted for inflation. The information is taken from building society advances for mortgages, and so may not reflect completely the overall market. Nevertheless, the prices are probably broadly indicative.

Table 10: Average House Prices 1981–91 (£)

	New dwellings	All dwellings
1981	28,119	24,188
1982	28,205	23,644
1983	30,817	26,471
1984	33,080	29,106
1985	36,103	31,103
1986	43,562	36,276
1987	49,692	40,391
1988	61,873	49,355
1989	73,544	54,846
1990	75,037	59,785
1991	73,507	62,455

Source: *Housing and Construction Statistics*

There are marked regional variations in property prices in Britain. In general, property is most expensive in London and is cheaper in the regions further away from the South East. In 1991, average prices for dwellings varied from £85,700 in Greater London to £35,400 in Northern Ireland.

Government research[5] has established a link between house prices and the release of land for housing. This found that land supply responds to market pressure and in turn affects housing supply and house prices. Housing land prices rose even faster than house prices over the period 1968-88. Planning permission is an important influence on the process; generally, faster processing of planning applications has contributed to the supply of housing land responding faster to increased demand.

Finance

Few people have sufficient savings to be able to afford the price of a house straight away. Most therefore buy their homes with a mortgage loan, with the property as security. Building societies have traditionally been the largest source of such loans, although banks, specialist mortgage companies and other financial institutions now take a significant share of the mortgage market. The share of gross advances made by building societies declined from 89 per cent in 1980 to 67 per cent in 1991. Some companies, especially in the financial services sector, also make loans for house purchase available to their own employees. Building societies raise funds for mortgage loans by taking deposits from savers. The interest paid on the mortgage loans can then provide for paying interest to depositors. Building societies are regulated by the Government under the Building Societies Act 1986. A Building Societies Commission has been established to oversee their activities. Under the legislation, building societies are now permitted to change their status to banks if the depositors approve.

[5] See **Further Reading**, p. 80.

Mortgages

The amount that lenders are prepared to advance to a would-be house purchaser is generally calculated as a multiple of his or her annual income, typically up to two-and-a-half times earnings, and the term of the loan is commonly 25 years. The two main forms of mortgage are 'repayment' and 'endowment' mortgages. In the former, the borrower repays principal and interest on the sum outstanding. In the latter, he or she pays only interest to the lender but also puts money into an endowment policy, which on maturity provides a lump sum to repay the principal. Owner-occupiers get basic rate tax relief on interest payments on mortgages of up to £30,000 on their main home. Mostly this is handled under the MIRAS—Mortgage Interest Relief At Source—scheme. Under this, the mortgage lender reduces the monthly repayment by the level of the relief and reclaims the difference from the Government. About 90 per cent of mortgages are covered by this scheme, and total government expenditure on mortgage interest relief was over £6,000 million in 1991–92.

Interest rates charged by building societies fluctuate broadly in step with the base lending rate set by the Government, usually a little above it. The rates actually paid by borrowers change to a greater or lesser degree dependent upon the frequency of revision—some borrowers may have a fixed rate loan which is reviewed only at very long intervals, while other borrowers may have opted for a rate revalued at frequent intervals. Most people have loans that are adjusted once a year, so that changes in mortgage rates take some time to be reflected in payments by borrowers. Table 11 shows the average level of mortgage rates since 1985; rates fell to a low level in 1987–88, rose again from late 1988 onwards and have since fallen back considerably.

Table 11: Interest Rates 1985–1991

	Bank base rates	Building society basic mortgage rates
	Annual average, per cent	
1985	12.25	13.21
1986	10.90	11.83
1987	9.74	11.54
1988	10.09	10.97
1989	13.85	13.65
1990	14.77	15.12
1991	11.70	12.84

Source: *Building Societies Commission*

Mortgage Rescue Schemes

The high level of interest rates between 1988 and 1991 and the subsequent rise in unemployment led to an increase in mortgage arrears and repossessions. A package of measures to protect home-owners from unnecessary repossession was therefore announced by the Government in December 1991. These include provision for income support covering mortgage interest[6] to be paid directly to lenders, and agreement with the mortgage lenders on the introduction of schemes to help borrowers in difficulty to remain in their homes. These had a number of different aspects, including provisions for mortgages-to-rents, rescheduling, debt counselling and shared equity. In exchange for direct payment of income support, lenders confirmed that they would not repossess properties where

[6] Some people on income support are eligible for payments to cover the interest on their mortgage; in general it is mortgagers who become unemployed who receive this. The Government spent over £900 million on this in 1991.

mortgage interest payments were covered by income support payments.

In July 1992, the Government published estimates that the scheme would rescue 55,000 people, many more than had originally been forecast. There has been a rise in long-term arrears; this results at least in part from mortgage lenders increasingly avoiding repossessions. Figures published by the Council of Mortgage Lenders show that the number of properties taken into possession in the first half of 1992 was 8 per cent down on the second half of 1991.

Maintenance and Improvements

As well as expenditure on buying houses, owner-occupiers also spend considerable sums on maintenance and improvement of their property. The 1986 English House Condition Survey found that the value of work carried out by owner-occupiers in that year alone was £12,100 million, a real increase of over 30 per cent since 1981.

Low-cost Home Ownership

To help more people enjoy the benefits of owner-occupation, the Government is encouraging the provision of 'low-cost housing' — that is, housing made available for purchase to people in housing need. Such schemes can include shared ownership, whereby someone buys part of a property from a local authority or housing association and pays rent on the remainder.

There may be particular problems in rural areas in securing the provision of sufficient low-cost housing to ensure the continuing viability of some villages. Where there is an overriding need, local planning authorities may permit low-cost housing on sites not allocated for housing in their development plans and on which general housing would not normally be allowed. Any such housing should meet normal development control standards, for example, in terms of landscaping and access, and should not breach Green Belt policy.

Public Rented Housing

The public rented sector grew from virtually nothing during the course of the late nineteenth and twentieth centuries; previously, the vast majority of households in Britain rented their homes from private landlords or their employer. Such social housing as existed was provided by almshouses and, in the nineteenth century, by charitable bodies such as the Peabody Trust and the Guinness Trust. However, legislation such as the Artisans' and Labourers' Dwellings Act 1875 gave local authorities the power to make provision for housing in their areas, and large numbers of properties were erected. Later legislation gave them duties in relation to homelessness (see pp. 68–74).

Finance

Local authorities meet the capital costs of new house construction and of modernisation of their existing stock by:

—raising loans on the open market;

—borrowing from the Public Works Loan Board (an independent statutory body set up to make loans to local authorities);

—the use of part or all of the proceeds from the sale of local authority houses and other assets;[7] and

—contributions from their revenue accounts.

[7] Under the Local Government and Housing Act 1989, 50 per cent of the proceeds of the sale of non-housing assets, and 75 per cent of those of housing, must be retained to help pay off council debt; the remainder can be used for new capital spending, which could include housing. In Scotland, local authorities may use all the proceeds from the sale of their housing for new capital spending. In November 1992, the Chancellor of the Exchequer announced that between November 1992 and December 1993, all capital receipts could be used for new capital projects.

The Government annually issues credit approvals to local authorities. In England this is done under the Housing Investment Programme (HIP) system. Every year each council submits its HIP bid, which includes a strategy statement, a numerical appraisal and a request for capital allocations. Capital allocations are decided on the basis of these submissions. The Government is seeking to align more closely the bidding processes for local authority and housing association programmes. In Wales, allocation of credit approvals is partly determined by formula and partly in response to competitive bidding by councils, from which annual Housing Strategy and Operational Plan submissions are required.

Under the Local Government and Housing Act 1989, local authorities are obliged to maintain a separate housing revenue account (HRA). This is 'ring-fenced'; that is, money cannot be transferred from the council's main fund to meet a shortfall on the HRA, nor in general can a surplus on the HRA be used for non-housing purposes. This more closely relates the costs to tenants and the service provided. However, some of a council's housing functions, such as dealing with homelessness, are paid for outside the HRA.

The Government provides local authorities in England and Wales with housing revenue account subsidy, worth more than £3,700 million in 1992–93. In Scotland, housing support grant of £47 million is available for 1992–93. The Northern Ireland Housing Executive is financed on a similar basis to local authorities in Great Britain; in 1991–92 it received total government grant of £173 million in respect of all its varied functions.

Housing Benefit

The Government makes help with the cost of rents available to eligible tenants. Rather than subsidise the level of rents, this help is concentrated on eligible tenants through the housing benefit system.

People whose incomes are below certain specified levels may receive housing benefit equivalent to the full level of their rent. Factors that influence these levels include marital status, the number of children in the household and whether there are any other adults living in the household. Those whose savings are above a certain level (currently £16,000) are not eligible. Housing benefit is payable both to tenants in the public sector and to those who rent from a private landlord or housing association. If the tenant chooses, arrangements can be made for the money to be paid direct to the landlord. The Government spent some £5,600 million on housing benefit in Great Britain in 1991–92.

Tenants' Rights

Local authority tenants have various rights, largely derived from housing legislation, principally the Housing Act 1985, which consolidated many existing provisions. The rights that local authority tenants enjoy include:

—security of tenure;

—the publication of a free summary of the allocation rules;

—the right to a written tenancy agreement, and a rent book for those who pay their rent weekly;

—a right to succession—that is, for the family of the original tenant to take over the tenancy on his or her death;

—the Right to Repair, which enables tenants to do repairs if the council fails to do them itself and reclaim the cost of this from the local authority;

—the right to take in lodgers, provided that the council is informed;

—the right to exchange homes with another tenant, except in certain circumstances, such as one of the addresses being larger than the proposed new tenant's reasonable needs;

—a duty on local authorities to send its tenants an annual report on its performance; and

—a right for tenants to have access to their personal files.

If tenants are dissatisfied with the council or believe that they have suffered some injustice, they can complain to their local councillor or Member of Parliament. There is also a Local Government Ombudsman to whom specific complaints of maladministration can be made. The Ombudsman can then make investigations of complaints and where it is found that the council concerned is at fault, the Ombudsman can make a recommendation that compensation is paid. The right to complain to a councillor or the Local Government Ombudsman is not confined to housing matters; it applies to all local government services. However, in practice a very high proportion of complaints do relate to housing.

In Northern Ireland, complaints are dealt with through the internal complaints procedure of the Northern Ireland Housing Executive. If a tenant remains dissatisfied, he or she can also have recourse to the Northern Ireland Commissioner for Complaints.

Allocations and Transfers

The efficient allocation of council housing and a smooth system for transferring between one property and another are important aspects of housing management. A research report published in

June 1992[8] found that there were 670,000 local authority or housing association homes with two or more bedrooms spare where children had grown up and left home. Of these, some 94,000 householders were willing to move straight away and another 80,000 within five years.

Allocations

Each local authority is responsible for drawing up its own rules for the allocation of council homes. It would typically maintain waiting lists of those who have applied to it for housing. The households on these lists would generally have their needs assessed by means of a points system which allocates varying numbers of points according to the circumstances of the household and the time spent on the list. Households with the most points would then be given priority for offers of accommodation. Local authorities are obliged by law to publish a summary version of their allocation rules, and to have a copy of the full rules available for inspection.

Transfers

Tenants often wish to transfer to different homes for various reasons. These might include wanting to move to a different part of the country for work reasons; harassment or disputes with present neighbours, or owing to under-occupation. Normally, rehousing within one council's area would be handled through the same system as for allocations to new tenants. Rehousing may be given in special circumstances—for example, in cases of medical need or because of harassment by other tenants. Councils may also operate other schemes to meet particular circumstances—for example, if an

[8] See **Further Reading**, p. 80.

unsatisfactory estate is to be demolished and redeveloped, the tenants there would be given offers of accommodation elsewhere.

Because tenants often want transfers to a different part of the country, following a November 1989 review the Government established HOMES, a mobility scheme, by merging three existing schemes. These were the National Mobility Office, the London Area Mobility Scheme and the Housing Association Liaison Project. Having incorporated the last-named project, HOMES can therefore assist tenants in the housing association sector. Under the scheme, a proportion of lettings are available to tenants who wish to move areas. Councils must also allow tenants who wish to exchange accommodation with each other to do so, within certain limits. This is also the case where the tenants concerned live in different areas. To assist such exchanges between areas, a national government-run scheme, the Tenants' Exchange Scheme, was set up in 1982 to put tenants who wish to move to another part of the country in touch with tenants in that area who might wish to exchange with them.

Diversification of Tenure

The Government has introduced a number of schemes to diversify tenure within the publicly-rented sector and to enable more people to own their own homes. Especially important is the Right to Buy, but other initiatives have also been taken.

Right to Buy
The Right to Buy was originally introduced in 1980 under the Housing Act 1980 and the Tenants Rights Etc. (Scotland) Act 1980; these statutory provisions have since been amended and con-

solidated in subsequent legislation. Most local authority tenants who have rented from a public sector landlord for two years or more have the right to buy the home they live in, on freehold in the case of most houses and long leases in the case of flats or houses where the council itself has only a leasehold. There are certain exclusions, such as for dwellings adapted, or considered particularly suitable, for disabled or elderly people and for dwellings let in connection with work. Thus, for example, a schoolkeeper whose house was next to the school and who was required to live there as part of his job would not have a right to buy.

Purchasers under the scheme have the right to certain discounts on the purchase price they have to pay their local authority. For houses, this starts at 32 per cent for tenants of two years' standing and rises 1 per cent for each year of tenancy to a maximum of 60 per cent. In the case of flats, the discount starts at 44 per cent and rises by 2 per cent a year to a maximum of 70 per cent. There is, however, an upper limit of £50,000 for the discount for either type of property. Some or all of the discount has to be repaid if the property is sold within three years.

When a tenant applies to buy a property under the scheme, the local authority is required to make an offer price, which is its assessment of the market price less the entitlement to discount. Prospective purchasers who are dissatisfied with the offer can appeal to the independent Valuation Office agency for a definitive valuation. If the council is slow to process the application, the applicant has the right, after serving the appropriate notices, to have payments of rent set against the eventual purchase price. The Government has been concerned to reduce such delays, for example by requiring certain authorities to submit a monthly report. As a result there has generally been a noticeable reduction in delays.

For example, between September 1989 and September 1991 the number of Right to Buy cases held up beyond the statutory timescale in London boroughs fell from 13,300 to 2,200.

The Right to Buy scheme has proved very popular with tenants, and by October 1992 over 1.4 million local authority properties in Great Britain had been sold under it. This has made a significant contribution in the overall shift towards owner-occupation. Table 12 shows the number of sales under Right to Buy. The Northern Ireland Housing Executive operates a similar scheme, and had sold nearly 51,000 properties by March 1992.

Table 12: Applications and Sales under Right to Buy, Great Britain

	Applications	Sales completed
1980	n.a.	568
1981	n.a.	79,430
1982	186,522	196,430
1983	150,445	138,511
1984	148,614	100,149
1985	136,118	92,230
1986	172,683	89,250
1987	249,281	103,309
1988	386,863	160,568
1989	238,286	181,367
1990	140,680	126,210
1991	120,664	73,458

n.a. = not available   Source: *Housing and Construction Statistics*

Defective Housing

Some of the system-built properties sold under the Right to Buy scheme have turned out to have serious inherent structural defects.

Some properties suffered a substantial loss in value as a result of the defects, and building societies and other mortgage lenders became reluctant to advance money against such properties, so that it was very difficult for the owners to sell their homes. The Government therefore introduced help for people caught in this situation in the Housing Defects Act 1984 (now part of the Housing Act 1985), and equivalent legislation for Scotland. There is also similar legislation for Northern Ireland.

Eligible owners of houses built with systems designated as defective, bought before the defects became generally known, are entitled to 90 per cent grant from their local authority (or 100 per cent grant in cases of hardship) to help with the cost of reinstating the property to a satisfactory and mortgageable condition. This may include demolition and rebuilding. In England, there are 24 such systems designated, and in Scotland there are nine approved repair systems. If it is not feasible or economic to reinstate the house, owners are entitled to have the local authority repurchase it at 95 per cent of its defect-free value. Eligible owners have ten years in which to apply for assistance, and most should have been helped by the end of 1994–95.

Rents to Mortgages
Not all tenants have the financial standing to buy their home under the Right to Buy. To extend the number of tenants who can afford to buy their own home, the Government intends to introduce a statutory Rents to Mortgages scheme, following pilot schemes for new-town tenants in Basildon and Milton Keynes. Provisions in the Housing and Urban Development Bill, which was introduced into Parliament in October 1992, would enable tenants to buy their homes on payment of an initial sum, which must be at least the

amount they can afford to borrow on a mortgage and with repayments equivalent to their present rent. They would then be able to increase their share by further voluntary payments, although they need not pay off the remainder until resale. The scheme would be open to all secure tenants who have the Right to Buy, and who have not been in receipt of housing benefit in the previous 12 months.

In April 1991 Scottish Homes' Rents to Mortgages scheme, under which tenants can become homeowners for an initial payment which can be financed by a mortgage with payments similar to their rent, was extended to local authority tenants.

In Wales tenants of the Development Board for Rural Wales have a similar experimental scheme, called flexi-ownership, which was introduced in 1989. The fiftieth sale under this scheme was concluded in February 1992. Additionally, of the 850 tenants eligible for the scheme, some 35 had made enquiries about it by that time.

Tenants' Choice
The 'Tenants' Choice' provisions were introduced in the Housing Act 1988. Under these stipulations, if tenants on a council estate so wish, they can opt for a new landlord to take over the estate. This landlord could be a housing association, a private company or a co-operative run by the tenants themselves; however, the new landlord has to be approved first. In England, the Housing Corporation is responsible for approving prospective new landlords for council tenants under the Tenants' Choice provisions; in Wales, Housing for Wales has this responsibility. If a proposal to transfer is made, it has to be put to a ballot of the tenants and can then proceed unless a majority vote disapproves it; generally those tenants who wish to remain with the local authority as their landlord can do so.

Many council estates have a backlog of repairs, often requiring great sums of money, that could deter potential new landlords from wishing to take over the ownership of an estate. Where an estate which is being transferred to a new landlord is in poor condition, therefore, the local authority can be required to pay a 'dowry' or disposal cost to the new landlord to cover the cost of essential repairs.

The first vote under the scheme to transfer ownership was held in October 1991, when tenants of two estates in Westminster voted to transfer to a resident-led company. Over four-fifths of tenants took part in the ballot; some 72 per cent were in favour of the proposal. Ownership of the estate has been transferred to a new company, with a housing association employed as managing agent. Owing to the poor condition of the estate, the District Valuer decided that a dowry of £17.5 million should be paid by Westminster City Council.

It can be a considerable burden for a group of tenants to take on the running of their estate. To help interested tenants obtain the necessary skills, therefore, the Government supports study courses. For example, in September 1992 a new bursary scheme was announced to support those studying with the Institute of Housing for the National Certificate in Tenant Participation. The Tenant Participation Advisory Service works with the Government to disseminate information on tenant participation. For example, they recently jointly produced *Tenants Together*, a booklet on the various forms of tenant participation available.

Other Sales

Although about 90 per cent of the houses and flats sold by local authorities to individuals are sold to sitting tenants, they also sell to other first-time buyers. These sales can be made at a discount on market value. Run-down properties are also sold by authorities to private individuals or developers for refurbishment and onward sale into owner-occupation or for renting. Local authorities not only sell existing stock but also build—usually in partnership with developers or housing associations—for sale to first-time buyers. By contributing land free or cheaply, they are able to sell the completed properties for up to 30 per cent less than market value and are able to sell them on shared ownership terms. These initiatives resulted in the completion of about 8,000 homes in 1991.

Cash Incentive Schemes

Under cash incentive schemes, existing council tenants can receive a grant to help them buy a home on the open market. Their council accommodation is thereby released for reletting to those in housing need. A government review of the first two years of cash incentive schemes was published in May 1992. It showed that in 1989–90, the first year of operation, 40 local authorities ran schemes paying 382 grants totalling £4 million. The second year showed even greater activity: 91 local authorities ran schemes paying 1,453 grants totalling £23 million; 1,130 properties had been released as a result of the extra funding under the Government's Homelessness Initiative (see p. 69). A total of 110 local authorities ran schemes and 3,185 grants were paid totalling £53 million. By the end of October 1992 over £21 million was available nationally for cash incentives in 1992–93. A further £30 million is being made available to local authorities in London and the South East for schemes in 1992–93.

In Wales, one scheme was approved in Cardiff in 1990–91; two further schemes in Wales were approved in 1991–92, with another scheme under consideration for 1992–93. Individual grants have been up to a maximum of £10,000. A requirement of all the schemes is that the houses released must be made available to homeless families.

Improved Management

The Government has taken or is taking a number of steps to improve the ways that local authorities manage their housing stock. An important part of this is a new Tenant's Charter, launched in England in January 1992.

Compulsory Competitive Tendering

A large number of local authority services, such as street sweeping, refuse collection and the management of leisure facilities, were subjected to compulsory competitive tendering (CCT) by the Local Government Act 1988. This meant that councils could not simply keep the work with their own workforces but were obliged to seek alternative tenders to see if the private sector could do the work more efficiently.

It was announced in April 1991 that CCT would be extended to the management of local authority housing stock; this was included as part of the Citizen's Charter launched in July 1991. The aim is to require councils to bring in managers who can demonstrate their ability to deliver the best services to tenants. Present local government legislation already allows for CCT to be applied to housing management, but the Government believes that some consequential and facilitative amendments should first be made to housing legislation; these are being introduced. It is proposed that, once this legislation takes effect, local authorities would

Priory Quay, a development of 33 homes around a yacht basin near Christchurch Priory in Dorset, is situated where the River Stour joins the Avon. Designed by the Cheshire Robbins Design Group, it won a Civic Trust award in 1990.

The Anchor Brewhouse is next to Tower Bridge, one of London's landmarks. Its conversion into residential use, designed by Pollard Thomas & Edwards Architects, was recognised by a Civic Trust award in 1991.

Pollard Thomas & Edwards

Housing associations are the main providers of new social housing. The Family Housing Association developed these homes for families and elderly people at Hafren Court in Cardiff.

This scheme at Dunmurry, near Belfast, won a regional award in the 1991 Design Award Scheme sponsored by the Royal Institute of British Architects.

Department of the Environment

Tenants in Hull meet with the staff of the Housing Action Trust (see p. 60) at a planning weekend to have their say on improvement plans.

Consultation with tenants is an important part of housing management. The Northern Ireland Housing Executive launched *Housing News*, a performance statement in the style of a newspaper, in 1991.

Department of the Environment

Houses in the Hartcliffe and Withywood area of Bristol, structurally sound but hard to heat in winter, being improved under the Green House Programme (see p. 63). Modifications include loft and floor insulation and double glazing.

Department of the Environment

Rundell Tower, a 22-storey tower block in Lambeth, south London, also benefitted from the Green House Programme. Improvements include new external cladding, heat recovery ventilation and a control system linked to weather sensors.

have up to five years to implement CCT, depending upon the size of their stock. Local authorities would be free to decide the size of their contracts, but the Government believes that these should be based on decentralised units such as individual estates.

In July 1992, it was announced that six local authorities were to run a pilot CCT scheme for their housing management. These authorities have been chosen to represent a broad cross-section of different councils. More authorities may join the pilot scheme in due course.

Under the proposal to put out to tender the management of local authority housing, tenants will have the opportunity to set up tenants' management organisations to bid for the running of the estate.

Tenant's Charter

The original Tenant's Charter was launched in 1981. It embodied important new statutory rights for tenants that were included in the Housing Act 1980. Following the launch of the Citizen's Charter in July 1991, a revised Tenant's Charter was published in January 1992. Local authorities in England have been asked to distribute leaflets to their tenants telling them about it. The new Charter sets out the rights that council tenants have, and gives guidelines for good practice in the way that local authorities manage their housing stock. It also sets out the Government's proposals further to improve the management of council housing and enhance the rights of council tenants. These include:

—an improved Right to Repair, which will mean that, instead of having to find the money to do the repair first and then reclaim it from the council, the bill can be sent direct to the local authority;

—new Right to Improve, which will entitle tenants to claim compensation for certain improvements which they carry out to their homes;

—publication of league tables, to be compiled by the Audit Commission,[9] comparing the performance of different councils according to standards it has laid down;

—the introduction of CCT into local authority housing management; and

—a new simple form of court action specifically to deal with disputes about housing rights.

A Tenant's Charter has also been published in Scotland, aimed at tenants of local authorities, new towns and Scottish Homes. Tenants' Charters have also been published for local authority tenants in Wales (in September 1992) and the tenants of the Northern Ireland Housing Executive. A copy of the new Charter has been delivered to all council tenants in Wales.

Training

The Government makes grants available under the Housing and Planning Act 1986 to support training in housing management. Bodies to have benefited include the Institute of Housing and the Local Government Training Board. A substantial part of this assistance also goes to tenant management initiatives. New criteria for these grants were announced in January 1991, which aim to target assistance at organisations which can best fill the gaps in other

[9] The Audit Commission is the government body that supervises the finances of local authorities and health authorities in England and Wales and appoints auditors to scrutinise their annual accounts.

provision and can train people in the skills needed by housing managers. In Scotland, similar grants are made under the Housing (Scotland) Act 1987.

Housing Associations

Housing associations are non-profit-making bodies that provide and manage homes for rent. They normally cater for people who would otherwise look to their local authority for a home; some groups provide particularly for the needs of special groups such as frail elderly, or disabled people. Most associations employ staff, but some rely on the work of volunteers. As well as buying properties and building new homes for rent, they also provide homes for sale through special schemes to help people on lower incomes wishing to become owner-occupiers. Housing associations also manage a large number of hostels.

The housing association movement is regulated under legislation such as the Housing Associations Act 1985. Government support to housing associations is substantial and has risen rapidly in recent years; this support is channelled through the Housing Corporation and its equivalents. The housing association movement is now the main provider of new social housing in Britain; in 1991 for the first time more properties were completed in Great Britain for housing associations than for local authorities.

Housing associations are very diverse in their composition, size, and structure. They are increasingly working in partnership with the local authorities, which retain statutory responsibility for homelessness provision in their areas. Such collaboration might take the form of a housing association buying surplus land from a council and developing it, paying part of the purchase price not in cash but by giving the local authority nomination rights to the completed properties. Housing associations are acquiring considerable experience in co-operating with local authorities to ensure that the optimum use is made of housing association grant (HAG) by releasing inner city land or by ensuring that scarce development land in rural areas is directed to housing. Many of these homes are allocated to people who are statutorily homeless, often as a result of local authorities utilising nomination rights.

Housing associations are also increasingly working in partnership with private developers, enabling funding to be arranged in new and radical ways to support large capital investment ventures. Associations can often bring management expertise to multi-tenure schemes. The Government also aims to increase the amount of private finance being used by housing associations, allowing significantly more homes to be built with the available public resources than would otherwise be the case.

Government Support

In Great Britain housing schemes carried out by housing associations qualify for HAG if the association concerned is registered with the Housing Corporation, Scottish Homes or Housing for Wales. These three organisations are statutory bodies which supervise housing associations in their respective parts of Great Britain and pay grant to assist them in their programmes. In Northern Ireland, housing associations registered with the Department of the Environment for Northern Ireland qualify for HAG.

Housing Corporation

The Housing Corporation promotes and supports the 2,300 registered housing associations in England; prior to April 1989 its functions also extended to Scotland and Wales. It is also responsible for regulating housing associations to ensure their proper management, for example, by requiring approval for their plans to borrow from private sector sources of finance.

Housing associations in England own, manage and maintain over 650,000 homes and some 60,000 hostel bed-spaces, providing homes for well over a million people. Over 25,000 additional homes for rent or shared ownership were provided in 1991–92. The Government increased the resources distributed to housing associations through the Housing Corporation's capital programme from £935 million in 1989–90 to £1,770 million in 1992–93.

The Housing Corporation's major objectives for its regulatory role are to:

—safeguard past and future public investment in housing associations, and ensure its prudent stewardship;

—ensure that housing associations comply with statutory and other regulatory requirements;

—ensure that housing associations are sound vehicles for public and private investment aimed at meeting the need for social housing; and

—ensure that the tenants of housing associations receive a good service from their landlords in line with the requirements of the Tenants' Guarantee.

The Corporation is increasingly looking to conduct regular reviews and to target its visits on particular problem areas in individual associations, rather than mounting full-scale monitoring visits every few years. Special attention is paid to monitoring new associations.

Housing for Wales

Housing for Wales (Tai Cymru) was established in April 1989 to take over the functions of the Housing Corporation in Wales. It aims to increase the supply of well-managed, good quality housing in Wales for those unable to meet their needs through purchase or renting at open market prices, and to do so in ways which provide good value for money. It also has the responsibility for overseeing in Wales the operation of the Tenants' Choice provisions of the Housing Act 1988, enabling local authority tenants to choose a new landlord.

Housing for Wales is managing a programme of over £180 million in 1992–93, with a target of providing over 4,000 additional new homes in Wales. It works closely with the Welsh Federation of Housing Associations, and consults widely with other relevant interest groups. It also liaises regularly with each of the district councils in Wales, in particular to ensure that new housing is targeted towards locations and client groups with the highest priority need. On current plans, government provision to the housing association movement in Wales will be over £500 million between 1991–92 and 1994–95. There are 107 registered housing associations in Wales, of which 36 have active development programmes. It has closely studied the range of housing problems in Wales and established a variety of measures, including the Village Initiative, to tackle these. Up to 10 per cent of its programme is targeted towards those in special need, such as women seeking refuge from domestic violence and people with mental health problems.

Scottish Homes

Scottish Homes was also set up in April 1989 to take over the functions of the Housing Corporation in Scotland, and has a wide range of general functions. On its establishment, it absorbed the Scottish Special Housing Association, which directly provided some 75,000 homes for rent. Scottish Homes intends to shed its landlord role to concentrate on its enabling functions. By March 1992 the number of houses it managed had fallen to 62,000 through Right to Buy sales and voluntary transfers. There are some 220 housing associations in Scotland registered with Scottish Homes. Its total programme expenditure in 1992–93 is expected to be about £333 million, of which over half will go to housing associations.

Scottish Homes has been given a major role in tackling housing-related urban dereliction and providing rural housing opportunities, in co-operation with local communities, the private sector, local authorities and other statutory agencies. Some groups of tenants are joining together to form community-based housing associations and tenant ownership co-operatives.

Northern Ireland
The Department of the Environment for Northern Ireland registers, promotes and supervises the 46 registered housing associations in Northern Ireland, which between them manage nearly 12,000 homes. The 45 associations which build for rent will between them spend about £43 million in 1992–93 to provide a planned 900 new homes. In addition, the Northern Ireland Co-Ownership Housing Association, which administers an equity-sharing scheme, has £7.5 million to meet expected demand from some 550 applicants. From 1993–94 associations will be working to a new development strategy devised in partnership with the Northern Ireland Housing Executive. One-third of future programmes will be targeted towards those in special needs categories.

Other Support

As well as HAG paid through the statutory bodies, the Government supports the work of housing associations in other ways, particularly through the funding that it makes available for urban regeneration. For example, work is under way in Newcastle upon Tyne on an £18 million project to provide 613 homes; provision for this is made up of £11 million through HAG and £7 million from the government-funded Tyne and Wear Development Corporation. Other government urban regeneration grants and programmes that assist the work of housing associations include City Grant, the Urban Programme and City Challenge (see pp. 63–5).

Tenants' Guarantee

In England and Wales the rights of housing association tenants are protected under the Tenants' Guarantees, which are issued by the Housing Corporation and Housing for Wales. They cover matters such as tenancy terms, principles for determining rent levels and the allocation of tenancies. Under these guarantees, tenants receive contractual rights in addition to their basic statutory rights, and associations are required to set and maintain rents at levels within the reach of people in low-paid employment. In Scotland, similar non-statutory guidance, in the form of a model tenancy agreement, has been implemented as proposed jointly by Scottish Homes and the Scottish Federation of Housing Associations.

The Housing Corporation launched a new Tenant Participation Strategy in July 1992 to encourage an increase in tenant involvement in housing management. This strategy put forward several proposals, including:

—revisions of performance criteria to encourage housing associations to give a greater say to their tenants, especially through delegated management;

—co-operation with the Department of the Environment to set up an ombudsman service to improve the handling of tenants' complaints;

—extension of the range of participation options open to tenants; and

—three-year regional tenant participation strategies, setting out targets and requirements for resources.

Large-scale Transfers

In recent years, some local authorities have decided to divest themselves of their housing stock by transferring it to housing associations, often set up for that purpose. The consent of the relevant Secretary of State[10] is required for this to go ahead, and guidelines were published for this in 1988. These state that consent would be unlikely for disposal to a body in which the local authority concerned had more than a 20 per cent stake, and that a commitment would normally be required from the new landlord to re-let vacant dwellings at rents which are in reach of those in lower-paid employment. As the Government does not want large public sector monopolies to be transformed into large private sector monopolies, it has stated that consent is unlikely to be given for the disposal of more than 5,000–10,000 properties to a single purchaser.[11] By law, moreover, the tenants have to be consulted, and the transfer cannot

[10] In England, this is the Secretary of State for the Environment, and in Scotland and Wales the Scottish and Welsh Secretaries of State respectively.

[11] In Wales, the limit set was 4,000.

go ahead if a majority of tenants oppose it. Their Right to Buy is also preserved.

District councils which have carried out such transfers include Broadlands, Chiltern, East Dorset, Newbury, Sevenoaks, Swale, and Tonbridge and Malling. In the light of the experience of these and other authorities, in November 1992 the Government issued a consultation paper on revision of the existing criteria for consent and on the financial arrangements for transfer. This proposed:

—a lowering of the size limits on individual transfers;

—a new requirement that all new landlords should have to be registered housing associations;

—legislation to allow the Government to limit the number of transfers taking place each year; and

—a requirement for local authorities to pay a levy on the price received where this exceeded the associated debt.

Rural Housing

Housing associations are playing a key role in providing low-cost housing in rural areas, often working in partnership with local authorities and the private sector. Selective relaxations of planning regulations where need can be clearly demonstrated are helping this process. In England, the Housing Corporation has provided funding for 4,600 such dwellings since 1990, and plans to fund the building of over 4,600 more by 1995. The Government has provided some £50 million of additional support to over 100 English local authorities since 1991, and is committed to providing some £30 million more in 1992–93. It is hoped that this will lead to the provision of about 2,500 further low-cost dwellings by the end of 1993. Similar schemes have been implemented in other parts of Britain. For example, details were announced in May and October 1992 of a special allocation of £4 million to Welsh local authorities to develop some 166 homes in rural Wales, mostly through co-operation with local housing associations. In September 1990, Scottish Homes launched a range of initiatives on rural housing as part of its Rural Strategy, and considerable progress is being made through these. In 1991–92, 626 units received approval; by the end of March 1992, 290 homes had been completed. An additional allocation of £3.3 million has been made to Scottish Homes in 1992–93 to investigate ways of bringing empty houses back into use; priority is being given to initiatives including the Scottish Landowners' Federation and the Forestry Commission. In September 1992 the Rural Housing Association was launched in Northern Ireland; it is specifically dedicated to tackling poor quality housing in rural areas.

Private Rented Housing

Private renting used to be the major form of tenure in Britain, but has declined markedly during this century. The Government seeks to revive the private rented sector so as to provide more choice in housing tenure. Low-income private tenants, like those in the local authority and housing association sectors, are entitled to financial help with their rent in the form of housing benefit. The law forbids landlords to harass their tenants as a way of trying to evict them.

A survey carried out for the Department of the Environment in 1990[12] found that 1.6 million households in England—some 8.5 per cent of the total—were renting from private landlords, including employers. This represents a relatively small decline since 1988, when the comparable figure had been 8.8 per cent. There were 483,000 tenancies of the new deregulated types created under the Housing Act 1988 (see p. 54), almost balancing the decline of 478,000 tenancies of the old sorts which could no longer be created. The survey also found that:

—the proportion of tenancies which had been created recently was higher than in 1988;

—the proportion of younger tenants was higher, and that of older tenants lower, than in 1988; and

—the average weekly rent for all types of tenancy was £43 in 1990, while for assured tenancies and assured shorthold tenancies average rents were £61 and £66 respectively.

[12] See **Further Reading**, p. 80

In Scotland, an estimated 189,000 dwellings were rented from private landlords and housing associations in December 1991.

Deregulation

The Housing Act 1988 and its Scottish equivalent, the Housing (Scotland) Act 1988, introduced two new forms of tenancy—assured tenancies and assured shorthold tenancies.[13] The first gives the tenant long-term security of tenure for a market rent freely negotiated between tenant and landlord. The second form is for a fixed term at a rent to be negotiated. The tenant of a shorthold tenancy, however, is able to apply at any time during the initial period of the tenancy to a rent assessment committee for the rent to be determined. This committee is empowered to reduce the rent if it proves to be excessive in relation to other shorthold market rents in the same area. Tenancies under the Rent Act 1977, which existed at the time the Housing Act 1988 was passed, were unaffected; they continue on the previous basis.

'Rent-a-Room' Scheme

The Government introduced its Rent-a-Room scheme by including provisions in the Finance Act 1992. These are effective from the 1992–93 tax year, allowing householders to receive income of about £65 per week from letting rooms in their homes to lodgers free of tax. The new relief applies to owner-occupiers and tenants who let furnished accommodation in their only or main home. Gross annual payments from such lettings which do not exceed £3,250 a year are now exempt from income tax altogether. Those who receive payments over £3,250 can choose between paying tax

[13] In Scotland, this is called a short assured tenancy.

on the excess amount without any reliefs for allowable expenses, or calculating their profit (namely gross rent less actual expenses) and paying tax on the profit in the normal way. It is estimated that the present cost of the scheme to the Exchequer will be between £2 million and £3 million a year, but this is likely to increase as the scheme encourages more people to rent out rooms.

Housing Association Schemes

In September 1992, the Government announced that a programme to bring vacant private sector houses back into use would be expanded to cover the whole country, following the success of five pilot schemes launched in August 1991. The HAMA pro-gramme—Housing Associations as Managing Agents—allows landlords to hand over tenant management responsibilities to hous-ing associations. The aims of the schemes are to persuade the own-ers of empty properties to bring them back into use, to attract new landlords into private letting, and to benefit homeless people who rent the properties. The Government plans to make £1.25 million available through the Housing Corporation to set up these schemes across England.

A total of £5.5 million was allocated by the Government in May 1992 to support schemes to increase and improve private rented accommodation in Wales. The money, which is being made available through local authorities, supports schemes which involve housing associations working directly with landlords.

Home Improvement and Rehabilitation

In urban areas of Britain slum clearance and redevelopment used to be major features of housing policy, but there has been a trend in recent years towards the retention of existing communities, accompanied by the modernisation and conversion of sub-standard homes. The number of houses demolished in clearance programmes has therefore declined markedly in recent years.

Housing conditions have improved considerably, but there are still areas where there are concentrations of dwellings which are unfit or which require substantial repairs. In such circumstances, local authorities are encouraged to consider improvement on an area-wide basis, coupling housing renovation and renewal with economic regeneration of the locality. Several government programmes exist to improve housing conditions in the public and private sectors.

Home Renovation Grants

Home improvement grants worth over £4,517 million were paid in respect of over 1.3 million privately owned dwellings in England alone between 1981 and 1991. In Wales, some 204,000 houses were grant-aided at a cost of £621 million. A new house renovation grant system was introduced in England and Wales in July 1990. Under this system, local authorities give mandatory renovation grants to enable unfit dwellings to be brought up to a revised fitness standard, with discretionary grants available for a wider range of works. Grants of up to 100 per cent may be available, subject to a test of the applicant's resources.

Grants are also available in certain circumstances for the provision of facilities for the disabled and for the repair of houses in multiple occupation and of the common parts of blocks of flats. Minor works assistance is also available to help people in receipt of income-related benefits with small-scale works.

The grant system in Scotland differs from that in England and Wales; grant is in the main discretionary and average rates range between 50 and 75 per cent. Improvement grants cover a wide range of work which may be needed to improve houses. Repair grants may be made towards works which if neglected would threaten the useful future life of the house. About £1,017 million was paid out in respect of some 352,000 houses between 1980 and 1990 in Scotland. Scottish Homes also has the power to provide grants to complement the role of local authorities in private house renewal.

In Northern Ireland, improvement and repair grants are available through the House Renovation Grants scheme, administered by the Northern Ireland Housing Executive. While broadly similar to that operating in England and Wales, it provides an additional facility to assist the replacement of unfit housing in isolated rural areas.

Renewal Areas

Renewal areas in England and Wales are intended to provide a focus for area action, covering both renovation and selective redevelopment of predominantly private sector stock, and taking account of a range of issues wider than just housing. Authorities are free to declare renewal areas without the specific consent of the Secretaries of State for the Environment and for Wales, provided they fulfil certain criteria. These require the area to include at least 300 dwellings, 75 per cent of which are privately owned and are determined unfit.[14] Authorities have powers to acquire land in renewal areas and to carry out improvement works. Subsidy for works to improve the environment of up to £1,000 per dwelling in the area is available.

In Scotland, housing action area powers are available for the improvement of areas in which at least half the houses fail to meet a statutory tolerable standard. Since 1975, 1,845 housing action areas have been declared. Outside such areas in Scotland local authorities have powers to serve improvement orders to houses below the statutory tolerable standard or lacking certain standard amenities. Local authorities may also give grants towards improving the environment of predominantly residential areas.

Northern Ireland has a large number of houses which are either unfit or in serious disrepair. Since 1977, 53 housing action areas have been declared, involving a continuous programme of rehabilitation and associated environmental improvement schemes. In addition, the Northern Ireland Housing Executive undertakes a programme of improvement of its own stock.

Estate Action Programme

The Estate Action programme provides local authorities in England with additional resources to regenerate their run-down housing estates. Funds are provided to enable authorities to carry

[14] In Wales, the minimum size is 150 dwellings.

out an agreed package of measures on an estate, including physical refurbishment and improved management. In February 1992, government approval was announced for eight schemes with a total value of £16 million. These approvals took the total allocated or earmarked for the Estate Action programme since its inception to more than £1,000 million.

In 1992–93 funds have been increased to £364 million, an increase of more than one-third on the previous year's budget. The Government is looking in particular for schemes in which local authorities can show a strategic approach to promoting comprehensive regeneration; an effective partnership with tenants and the private sector; and that the investment in housing would complement and support training, enterprise and other urban policies.

A few of the many projects to have benefited from Estate Action include:

—a £420,000 contribution towards upgrading security at five tower blocks in Middlesbrough;

—a £2 million scheme to improve a 21-storey tower block in Newham, east London, by means of energy conservation measures and the introduction of a 'concierge' system;[15]

—a £5 million scheme to renovate the Browning estate in Southwark, south London, over four years, including improved security; and

—a £12 million programme on the New Loughborough estate in Brixton, south London, to remedy major disrepair including concrete spalling and water penetration.

---

[15] The 'concierge' system involves having a doorkeeper who controls access by strangers to the building; such schemes can be very effective in cutting back on crime and vandalism.

Homesteading

The Government is committed to introducing a pilot home-steading scheme as part of Estate Action, under which local authorities would be encouraged to offer those in housing need the chance to restore council properties in exchange for a reduced rent or the opportunity to buy at a reduced price.

Estate Partnership

Estate Partnership is a Welsh Office initiative which aims to bring improvements to the quality of the housing stock, and the lives of its occupants, on a co-ordinated and comprehensive basis. The first two local authority estates to benefit were announced in October 1992, some £5 million being allocated for one and £1.5 million for the other. Possible further funding is to be discussed with the local authorities concerned.

Housing Action Trusts

Housing Action Trusts (HATs) can be established in England and Wales to focus resources on some of the most run-down areas of predominantly local authority housing. The Government can designate a HAT for a particular area or estate, subject to a tenants' vote. If a majority of those tenants who vote support the proposal, the HAT would be established by parliamentary Order. It would take over responsibility for the housing in its designated area to renovate it, improve the environment, provide community facilities and stimulate local enterprise. On completion of its work, the HAT would be wound up and its property transferred to other owners and managers, such as housing associations or tenants' co-operatives, or back to the local authority. Tenants would be consulted on their future landlords. Tenants as well as local authorities may apply for the establishment of a HAT.

Two HATs have already been established, in Hull (Humberside) and in Waltham Forest (north-east London), and some tenants in Liverpool have also approved the establishment of a HAT on their estate. Under this proposal, a total of 35 tower blocks will have in excess of £100 million spent on them over a seven- to ten-year period. Further ballots are being held to seek approval for more HATs.

Home Improvement Agencies

A large number of home improvement agencies exist to help low-income, elderly or disabled people carry out repairs and improvements to their properties, by means both of advice and practical help. In many cases this enables people to remain in their own homes who would otherwise have had to move out. New arrangements for government funding were introduced in England in March 1991; the Government meets up to half the running costs of approved agencies, the money being channelled through local authorities. In 1992–93 such funding is being provided to 115 local authorities in England to help agencies in their area; total support is £3.5 million. In Wales, £546,000 has been made available for a similar initiative for 1992–93.

Flats Over Shops Initiative

There is a large amount of residential property above shops, much of which would originally have provided a home for the shop-keeper. With the major changes that have taken place in retailing patterns in recent decades, much of this has now become vacant.

In October 1991 the Government launched its Flats Over Shops initiative to bring this accommodation back into use. Some £25 million is being made available over three years to local authorities to enable them to assemble projects with housing associations and private shopkeepers to rehabilitate such property for letting to those in housing need; allocations of over £5 million were announced in May 1992. The Government also produces publicity aimed at encouraging commercial property owners to look at residential letting as a profitable use of their property. Several voluntary organisations, including the Living Over the Shop project, which is partially funded by the Government, are also involved in promoting such schemes.

In Wales, local authorities have promoted schemes to convert disused commercial accommodation into houses and to bring empty living accommodation above shops back into use. The schemes involve both renovation grants to owners and partnership arrangements with housing associations. Since May 1991, resources of more than £10 million have been issued to Welsh local authorities in support of these schemes.

Design Improvement Controlled Experiment

This initiative was launched in October 1990; it aims to improve the design of specific estates in ways that will make them less susceptible to vandalism and crime. Typical changes include removing networks of paths and alleyways, creating individual front entrances for small groups of flats, and turning open space into private gardens for ground-floor residents. These changes are agreed after extensive consultation with local tenants. Projects announced under the initiative include:

—a £4.5 million scheme on the Rogers estate in Tower Hamlets, east London;

—a £7.5 million scheme to turn the Bennett estate, Manchester, into a series of island sites surrounded by roads and to provide extra security for tower blocks; and

—a £3 million scheme for the Avenham estate in Preston to divide large low-rise blocks into smaller self-contained sections.

Green House Programme

The Government launched its 'Green House' programme to improve energy efficiency in local authority properties in England in December 1990. The 1992–93 allocation is some £45 million in the programme to date, which will go to 127 schemes split between 91 local authorities. Measures supported under the programme include the introduction of extra insulation, heat pumps, condensing boilers and sophisticated electronic controls. In Scotland, additional resources totalling £7.6 million have been made available in 1992–93 to 45 local authorities to support projects that demonstrate energy efficiency and saving measures.

Other Measures

There are other government programmes which, while not aimed specifically at housing problems, also make a contribution to the improvement of existing homes and the provision of new ones; this is particularly true of inner city areas.

City Challenge
The City Challenge initiative brings together the work of existing programmes and bodies to tackle the problems of run-down urban

areas. Local authorities in partnership with the private sector, local voluntary organisations and the community are invited to draw up imaginative and comprehensive programmes specifically designed to regenerate key areas over a five-year period. A total of £37.5 million has been made available to each of the first-round 'pacemaker' authorities for schemes beginning in 1992–93. A further 20 second-round competition winners have been invited to draw up their programmes for action and, if acceptable, they will commence work in 1993–94.

Urban Programme

The Urban Programme helps tackle the economic, environmental and social problems of targeted run-down areas. It provides support for a wide range of local authority, private and voluntary projects submitted by designated local authorities (of which there are 57 in England) as part of annual programmes of regeneration. In Wales, all local authorities are able to apply for funding from the Urban Programme. For capital projects, the Government pays 75 per cent grant and 25 per cent supplementary credit approvals. Revenue projects are funded through 75 per cent grant from the Government; local authorities make up the remainder from their own resources.

City Grant

City Grant is payable to support private sector developments in the 57 Urban Programme local authority areas in England. Many of the grants are for housing projects: as at the beginning of December 1992, City Grant of £67.4 million had been approved for 93 housing projects. These attracted £291 million of private sector investment to allow the construction of 8,610 homes and the reclamation of 183 hectares (453 acres) of vacant and derelict inner city land. The greatest number of homes to be built or refurbished in one single project is the development of Riverdale at Salford, where 483 new homes will be provided. The scheme involves the demolition of eight blocks of difficult-to-let local authority homes, the construction of 73 flats and 191 houses and the refurbishment of four tower blocks to provide an additional 220 flats for sale. A grant of £5.1 million was awarded towards the £31.3 million development so far undertaken.

The proposed Urban Regeneration Agency, which would be established by the Housing and Urban Development Bill, would take over responsibility for City Grant.

In Wales, Urban Investment grant is the equivalent of City Grant. Awards have ranged from £25,000 towards the cost of converting a chapel in Abertillery to provide five flats, to £3.5 million towards the regeneration of Tredegar town centre, including the provision of 70 houses.

Urban Development Corporations

Since the establishment of urban development corporations (UDCs) in 1981, there has been a continuing programme of housing development, aimed at all sectors of the housing market, within the UDC areas; the UDCs have encouraged private sector investment in housing in their areas. The Government has recently encouraged them to release more land for low-cost housing wherever possible. Up to the end of March 1992 over 21,600 housing units had been completed.

Urban Partnerships

In Scotland, Urban Partnerships have been established to direct the regeneration of four large peripheral housing estates situated in

Dundee, Edinburgh, Glasgow and Paisley. Their housing objectives include:

—providing greater choice through diversification of tenure and management;

—achieving a sustained improvement in the quality and supply of housing; and

—involving the tenants in the ownership and management of housing.

Slum Clearance

Local authorities have slum clearance powers, which are currently contained in the Housing Act 1985. Under these powers, they may issue compulsory purchase orders, issue demolition or closure notices and declare clearance areas. Houses acquired for clearance may be used as 'short life housing' to provide temporary accommodation. The Government pays slum clearance subsidy to meet 75 per cent of any losses incurred by local authorities in exercising their slum clearance functions in any year.

However, large-scale clearance programmes are now rarely considered necessary. Whereas in England in 1980–81 some 21,300 homes in or adjoining a clearance area were demolished, by 1990–91 this had fallen to 1,900. However, some 9,300 unfit homes were made fit in that year through renovations. In Scotland, 2,492 dwellings below the tolerable standard were demolished in 1979–80; this fell to 239 in 1989–90. In that year, 10,451 dwellings were improved to meet the standard, many more than in previous years.

Homelessness

The problem of homelessness is not confined to Britain; it is world-wide in its scope. Many advanced industrialised societies suffer from a degree of homelessness. The Government is taking a wide programme of measures to deal with the problem as it affects Britain. The reasons for homelessness are varied; it is estimated that in 1991 the main reasons given by applicants to local authorities were:

—that family or friends were no longer prepared to accommodate them (42 per cent);

—the breakdown of a marriage or other relationship with a partner (16 per cent);

—the loss of a private rented dwelling (27 per cent); and

—mortgage arrears (12 per cent).

Homelessness Legislation

The primary duty to assist homeless people, or those who are threatened with homelessness, falls upon local housing authorities. Legislation, currently embodied in the Housing Act 1985 and the Housing (Scotland) Act 1987, requires councils to assess the circumstances of people who present themselves to the council as homeless or threatened with it. Certain tests are used for this purpose:

—whether the applicants are without satisfactory accommodation or in imminent danger of losing their present accommodation;

—whether they are in one of the defined priority categories (such as families with young children, women expecting babies, and those vulnerable through old age, physical disability, mental handicap or illness); and

—whether they have a local connection with the area in which they apply.

The Northern Ireland Housing Executive has a similar duty under the Housing (Northern Ireland) Order 1988, although the last test does not apply in Northern Ireland.

If someone has left adequate housing and applies to a local authority as homeless, the authority could decide that the household has made itself intentionally homeless, which limits the responsibilities of the local authority. For households accepted as having a priority need, the local authority must offer temporary accommodation for a reasonable period. If the household is not in priority need, the council's duties are limited to the provision of advice. If, however, an authority accepts a household as unintentionally homeless and in priority need, it has a duty to secure permanent accommodation as quickly as possible, although it may need to use temporary accommodation first. There is also a duty to secure temporary accommodation for households who may be homeless and in priority need while the application is being investigated. If the applicant has no local connections, but does have a connection with the area of another local authority, responsibility for rehousing can be transferred to that other authority. In practice, however, this is rare, since most homeless people apply to their own local authority. About two-thirds of those found to be homeless and in priority need fell into the category of families with young children.

Steps that councils take permanently to house homeless people typically include making available a secure tenancy in their own stock or making a nomination through a housing association. Since it can take time to find permanent accommodation, various forms of temporary accommodation are also used. These can include hostels run by the council or other bodies, private sector properties leased on a short-term basis, and the use of bed-and-breakfast accommodation. The latter in particular is widely regarded as unsatisfactory, and many councils are taking steps to reduce or eliminate their use of it.

Homelessness Initiative

The number of people presenting themselves to local authorities as homeless has risen considerably in recent years, although recently this rise has slowed somewhat. Table 13 shows the number of enquiries carried out into households presenting themselves as homeless and the number found to be in priority need.

Table 13: Homelessness Enquiries and Acceptances by Local Authorities, Great Britain

	Enquiries	Acceptances
1983	170,190	75,470
1984	180,490	80,500
1985	203,480	91,010
1986	219,880	100,490
1987	227,730	109,170
1988	243,960	113,770
1989	252,290	122,180
1990	301,610	140,350
1991	302,690	144,530

Source: Department of the Environment

To combat the problem of homelessness, the Government launched its Homelessness Initiative in November 1989. This followed a review of the law on homelessness, which concluded that no legislative amendments were necessary. An extra £250 million was allocated to tackle homelessness in England over a two-year period. Of this, some £177 million went to local authorities and £73 million to housing associations. The aim of this funding was to secure extra accommodation, for example by allowing local authorities to renovate empty council properties and lease houses in the private sector for short-term accommodation. Other measures taken to combat homelessness include:

— an increase in the number of voluntary organisations in England receiving grants to help homeless people, up from 31 in 1990-91 (receiving £2 million) to 147 in 1992-93 (receiving £6.1 million); and

— a night-time and weekend telephone advice line, run by the housing charity Shelter, which was launched in November 1991.

Voluntary projects assisted by the Government vary widely in their scope. A large proportion of the help goes towards the provision of advice by organisations such as the Citizens' Advice Bureaux. Other projects assist young people who have moved to London to find accommodation in their home area, resettlement projects, and registers of lodgings.

To assist local councils further in dealing with homelessness, in July 1991 the Government also changed accounting rules on properties leased from the private sector for a short term. Where the lease is less than three years and the property is used for temporary accommodation for the homeless, the costs of the lease are dealt with outside the council's housing revenue account. This brought such leases into line with the costs of other forms of temporary accommodation.

Rough Sleeping

Most homeless people do not sleep rough, instead usually living in accommodation of some sort, even if it is substandard or temporary. As seen above, those in priority need and not intentionally homeless are rehoused by the local council, if only into temporary accommodation. It is therefore useful to draw a distinction between homelessness, which covers all those without permanent satisfactory accommodation, and rooflessness, which includes only those who do not have a roof over their heads. However, there are a minority of people who do sleep rough, especially in London, and the Government has made considerable efforts to reduce their numbers.

A Rough Sleepers' Initiative was launched in June 1990 with a budget of £96 million over three years. In November 1992 it was anounced that £86 million will be made available to extend the initiative until 1996. Measures taken to tackle the problem of rough sleeping include the creation of hostel spaces and the provision of more permanent move-on accommodation for people leaving the hostels. For example, a former Metropolitan Police section house in Hackney was converted into a hostel with space for 90 people; this opened in July 1992 and is managed by a housing association. Other voluntary organisations are also involved in the initiative by running the hostels that it has provided. Extra money has also been made available to local authorities to increase the number of places in flats and houses leased from private owners. Measures have also been taken to tackle particular problems—for example, in June 1992 it was announced that a special team of workers would help homeless people sleeping rough in the Lincoln's Inn Fields area, many of whom had drug or alcohol problems. These workers would concentrate on assisting individuals by finding accommodation suited to their needs and with recourse to the necessary counselling facilities.

By April 1992, the Government's programme of measures to tackle the problem of people sleeping rough in London had provided about 600 places in hostels and about 1,200 in move-on accommodation, with an additional 250 hostel places by mid-1992 and a further 1,300 permanent places by the end of 1993. It also made available money to fund provision of temporary winter shelters.

A survey carried out in March 1992 by voluntary organisations found 440 people sleeping rough in central London, much reduced on the 1,046 found by a similar survey in January 1991. The survey suggests that the Rough Sleepers' Initiative has been particularly successful in helping young people; of the 440 people found sleeping rough, only about 30 were aged 18 or less. The 1991 Census found 142 rough sleepers in Scotland's four cities, of whom 63 were in Edinburgh, and in Wales 29 rough sleepers were found on six identified sites.

Mentally Ill Rough Sleepers
A group especially targeted for help by the Government is mentally-ill people sleeping rough. An initiative to help this group was first announced in July 1990. In January 1992 it was announced that a further £8 million would be spent over three years to help this group, which would bring the total spent on the initiative to £20 million by 1994–95. Schemes assisted by this funding include the creation of short-term hostel places designed specially to meet the needs of people with a mental illness who had been sleeping

rough, and the provision by the Housing Corporation of 750 more permanent places as move-on accommodation for those leaving the specialist hostel places. Community psychiatric teams are also being funded to work with the homeless mentally-ill and encourage them to move into hostels.

Wales

Extra measures to deal with homelessness in Wales were announced in December 1989, shortly after the review of homelessness legislation. These included:

—a cash incentive scheme to help free existing council stock for re-letting to homeless people;

—consideration for a similar scheme for housing association tenants;

—additional consideration for schemes to relieve housing needs in Urban Programme approvals; and

—priority for issues of homelessness in deploying the Welsh Office's housing budget.

Since 1990–91 the government has made an extra allocation available to local authorities experiencing particular homelessness difficulties. They have been encouraged to submit bids involving innovative schemes in partnership with housing associations. In 1992–93 the Homelessness Reserve totalled over £4 million. Support to voluntary organisations helping homeless people has also been increased, amounting to £580,000 in 1992–93. The Government is also committing £800,000 over a three-year period to a pilot project in Cardiff which seeks to provide intensive social support for young, single, vulnerable homeless people to assist them in finding and holding onto permanent accommodation.

Scotland

Additional resources of some £15 million have been made available to local authorities in Scotland to fund projects to combat homelessness in their areas. The allocation of £7.5 million for 1992–93, which was announced in February 1992, will enable authorities to fund 44 different projects, including:

—an emergency short-stay hostel in Glasgow;

—the provision of furnished tenancies in Edinburgh and elsewhere; and

—follow-on accommodation for a stopover project in Clackmannan.

Overall, the allocation will enable accommodation to be provided for some 700 homeless people in 1992–93. Aid of about £1.5 million a year is paid to homelessness-related projects in Scotland under the Urban Programme. From April 1991, local authorities in Scotland which incurred deficits in running hostels have been able to qualify for additional housing-support grant.

Northern Ireland

The relief of homelessness in Northern Ireland is a responsibility of the Northern Ireland Housing Executive. Some 4,200 households were accepted as homeless and in priority need in 1991–92; as in Great Britain, this figure showed signs of the increase in applications tailing off. To accommodate homeless households, the Executive has provided ten hostels, with others planned. Working arrangements have also been established with a number of voluntary groups which provide accommodation, many of which are funded by the Executive.

Future Developments

Leasehold Reform

The Government announced its proposals for leasehold reform in July 1991. These reforms would give most leaseholders in a block of flats the right to buy the freehold of their block collectively at market price. To qualify for enfranchisement blocks would have to be predominantly residential with two-thirds of the flats let on long leases. At least two-thirds of these leaseholders would have to support enfranchisement before a buy-out of the freehold could take place. The valuation would reflect the market value of the landlord's freehold interest as well as an element of 'marriage value'— the extra value that comes from merging the freehold and leasehold interests. The leaseholders would become joint owners of the freehold in addition to retaining their leases. This would enable them to run the block instead of the landlord. Residents in blocks which did not qualify would instead be entitled to purchase a renewed lease. These measures form part of the Housing and Urban Development Bill.

Leasehold occupation, which is now largely confined to flats, used to be common for houses as well, but the Leasehold Reform Act 1967 gave leaseholders of houses with rateable values of less than £1,500 in London and £750 elsewhere the right to enfranchise—that is, buy the freehold of their property—and most have done so. Leasehold houses are now largely restricted to certain high-value properties (the current upper threshold on the enfranchisement provisions is an annual rental equivalent of £25,000), mainly in central London, which do not qualify for this. In March 1992, the Government announced proposals to abolish the upper limit, which would give leaseholders in high-value houses the same rights to buy their freeholds as other leaseholders.

New Settlements

There is a continuing need for new housing in Britain. However, both the extension of existing towns and villages and 'infill' development within them are often unpopular with the people who live there. Indeed, Green Belt planning policies exist, among other reasons, to stop existing towns sprawling and merging into one another.

One solution that has been put forward to accommodate the need for new housing, while at the same time avoiding the sprawl of existing towns and cities, is the creation of new settlements. These would be small towns built from scratch by private-sector developers, differing from the Government's post-war new town programme by the size of the settlements envisaged, and without recourse to special administrative structures such as a new town development corporation. A number of new settlements, ranging from small villages to small towns, have been proposed in recent years. Examples have included:

—Northwick, a proposal for a settlement of 4,000 houses and associated business and community facilities on Canvey Island (Essex);

—Great Lea, a proposal for up to 3,200 homes and a shopping centre south of Reading in Berkshire; and

—Foxley Wood, a proposal for 4,800 houses in Hampshire.

Many of the settlement proposals have been unpopular with local people. All the above examples were refused planning permission.

In the light of recent experiences, the Government issued fresh planning advice on new settlements in March 1992. This states that the Government does not reject the concept of new settlements, but to be successful a proposal for a new settlement would normally have to meet a number of requirements, that:

— the alternative of expanding existing towns or villages would represent a less satisfactory way of providing land for the new housing needed;

— the proposal is a clear expression of local preferences supported by local planning authorities;

— the proposed settlement would present no risk of unacceptable coalescence with existing settlements;

— the option of a new settlement, in preference to the alternative, would result in positive environmental improvements, for example through reclamation of derelict land, or upgrading of areas of low landscape value;

— the proposal can be considered alongside policies of restraint to protect the rejected alternative locations from development pressure; and

— it is not within a Green Belt, National Park, Area of Outstanding Natural Beauty, Site of Special Scientific Interest or on the best or most versatile agricultural land.

In this way the Government hopes that the net effect of a new settlement will either enhance the environment or cause only modest environmental impact which would be outweighed by the need to meet housing requirements. Guidance says that the need to respect local preference means that specific proposals for new settlements should normally only be promoted through the district-wide local plan or Unitary Development Plan.

Squatting

Squatting—the unauthorised and unlawful occupation of property —is at present largely a matter for the civil law. Only when the lawful occupier of the property is made homeless by squatters is the criminal law normally involved; otherwise the owner may regain his property through the civil courts. However, the Government is concerned that these existing remedies against squatters are slow and expensive, and in October 1991 it announced that it was consulting on squatting. The Government is presently considering, in the light of responses received, how the law might be improved.

Addresses

Department of the Environment, 2 Marsham Street, London SW1P 3EB.

Department of Health, Richmond House, 79 Whitehall, London SW1A 2NS.

Department of the Environment for Northern Ireland, Parliament Buildings, Stormont, Belfast BT4 3SS.

Scottish Office Environment Department, St Andrew's House, Edinburgh EH1 3DE.

Welsh Office, Cathays Park, Cardiff CF1 3NQ.

Housing Corporation, 149 Tottenham Court Road, London W1P 0BN.

Housing for Wales, 25-30 Lambourne Crescent, Llanishen, Cardiff CF4 5ZJ.

Northern Ireland Housing Executive, 2 Adelaide Street, Belfast BT2 8PB.

Scottish Homes, Thistle House, 91 Haymarket Terrace, Edinburgh EH12 5HE.

Council of Mortgage Lenders, 3 Savile Row, London W1X 1AF.

Institute of Housing, 9 White Lion Street, London N1 9XJ.

National House-Building Council, Buildmark House, Chiltern Avenue, Amersham HP6 5AP.

Further Reading

£

Mobile Homes in England and Wales: Report of a Postal Survey of Local Authorities, by Sarah Dyer. ISBN 0 11 752368 2.	HMSO	1991	6.00
Private Renting in England 1990, by Irene Rauta and Ann Pickering. ISBN 0 11 691444 0.	HMSO	1992	10.20
Houses into Flats: a Study of Private-Sector Conversions in London. Volume 1: Report of Main Findings, by John Sizer. ISBN 0 11 752675 4.	HMSO	1992	14.00
The Relationship between House Prices and Land Supply, prepared for the Department of the Environment by Gerald Eve Chartered Surveyors. ISBN 0 11 752593 6.	HMSO	1992	10.60
Underoccupation in Local Authority and Housing Association Housing, by Jill Barelli. ISBN 0 11 752639 8.	HMSO	1992	12.50

Annual Reports

Housing and Construction Statistics.   HMSO

General Household Survey.   HMSO

Building Societies Commission.   HMSO

The Housing Corporation.   The Housing
                                            Corporation

Index

Administrative arrangements 2, 4–5
Age of property 10
Amenities 1, 17–18
Audit Commission 42

Building societies 23, 24

Cash incentive schemes 39–40
City Challenge 49, 63–4
City Grant 49, 64–5
Compulsory competitive tendering 4, 40–1
Council housing *see* Public rented housing

Design Improvement Controlled Experiment initiative 62–3
Development Board for Rural Wales 37

Energy efficiency 63
English House Condition Survey 5, 7, 12, 17, 26
Environment, Department of the 5, 50, 53
Estate Action programme 5, 58–60

Flats Over Shops initiative 61–2

General Household Survey 7, 18
Government objectives 2, 3–4
Green House programme 63

Home improvement agencies 61
Homelessness 1, 5, 39, 67–74
HOMES mobility scheme 33
Homesteading 60
House prices 21–3

House-building 2, 8–9, 21
  construction methods 12
Housing Action Trusts 60–1
Housing and Construction Statistics 7
Housing associations 2, 3, 5, 13, 14, 16, 44–52, 55
Housing benefit 29–30, 53
Housing conditions (*see also* Rehabilitation of Housing)
  amenities and repair 1, 17–18
  housing stock 1, 7–13
  overcrowding 18–19
  tenure 13–17
Housing Corporation 5, 37, 44, 45–6, 47, 49, 51, 55, 73
Housing for Wales 37, 45, 47, 49
Housing Investment Programme 29
Housing revenue account 29
Housing Standards Company Ltd 21

Leaseholders' rights 4, 20–1, 75–6
Legislation 2, 3–4, 19, 21, 23, 28, 29, 30, 33–4, 36, 37, 40, 41, 42, 43, 44, 47, 54, 65, 66, 67, 75
Local government authorities (*see also* Public rented housing) 2, 4–5, 6, 21
  and homelessness 5, 67–74
  and housing associations 44–5, 50–2
  and housing rehabilitation 56–66
Local Government Ombudsman 31
Low-cost home ownership 26–7

Management of public sector housing 4, 40–3

Mentally ill rough sleepers 72–3
Mobile homes 12–13
Mortgages 23, 24–6
  Rents to Mortgages scheme 4, 17, 36–7
  rescue schemes 25–6
  tax relief on interest payments 3, 20, 24

National House-Building Council 21
New settlements 76–8
Northern Ireland, housing in
  action areas 58
  Department of the Environment 45, 48
  homelessness 74
  house prices 22
  housing stock 7
  public expenditure 1
  renovation grants 57
  rural housing 52
  statutory provisions 2, 36
  Tenants' Charter 42
  tenure 16
Northern Ireland Co-Ownership Housing Association 48
Northern Ireland Housing Executive 2, 5, 29, 31, 35, 42, 48, 57, 58, 68, 74

Overcrowding 18–19
Owner-occupied housing (*see also* Cash incentive schemes, Rents to Mortgages schemes *and* Right to Buy) 2, 3, 13, 14, 16–17
  finance 23–7
  maintenance and improvements 26
  prices 21–3
  types of ownership 20–1

Planning 6, 21, 23, 76–7
Prices *see* House prices

Private rented housing 2, 3–4, 13, 14, 16, 53–5
Properties
  age of 10
  types of 10–13
  vacant 17
Public expenditure 1, 5, 29, 30
Public rented housing 2, 3, 4–5, 13, 14, 16
  allocation and transfers 31–3
  diversification of tenure 33–40
  finance 28–30
  management 4, 40–3
  tenants' rights 30–1
Public Works Loan Board 28
Rehabilitation of housing 56–66
Renewal areas 57–8
Renovation grants 5, 56–7, 62
Rent a Room scheme 4, 54–5
Rented sector *see* Housing associations, Private rented housing *and* Public rented housing
Rents to Mortgages scheme 4, 17, 36–7
Research 5, 23
Right to Buy 3, 12, 13, 33–5
  defective housing 35–6
Right to Improve 42
Right to Repair 4, 30, 41
Rough sleeping 71–3
Rural housing 51–2

Scotland, housing in
  action areas 58
  energy efficiency 63
  homelessness 74
  housing stock 7, 10
  housing support grant 29
  legislation 2, 3–4, 19, 33–4, 36, 43, 54, 67
  private rented housing 54
  public expenditure 1

Scotland, housing in *continued*
  renovation grants 57
  Rents to Mortgages scheme 37
  rough sleeping 72
  rural housing 52
  slum clearance 66
  Tenants' Charter 42
  tenure 14, 16
  Urban Partnerships 65
Scottish Federation of Housing
  Associations 49
Scottish Homes 37, 42, 45, 47–8,
  49, 52, 57
Secretaries of State (for Scotland,
  Wales, Northern Ireland and the
  Environment) 2, 4, 50, 58
Sheltered housing 13
Slum clearance 66
Social housing *see* Housing
  associations
Squatting 78
Stamp duty 20

Tai Cymru *see* Housing for Wales
Temporary homes 12
Tenants' Charter 40, 41–2
Tenants' Choice 37–8, 47
Tenants' Exchange Scheme 33
Tenants' Guarantee 46, 49–50
Tenants' rights 30–1
Training in housing management
  42–3
Types of property 10–13

Urban Development Corporations 65
Urban Programme 49, 64, 74

Vacant property 17

Wales, housing in
  administrative arrangements 2
  amenities 18
  cash incentive schemes 39–40
  commercial accommodation
    conversion 62
  Estate Partnership 60
  flexi-ownership 37
  homelessness 73
  Housing Action Trusts 60–1
  Housing for Wales 37, 45, 47,
    49
  housing revenue account 29
  housing stock 7, 8, 10
  private rented housing 55
  renewal areas 57–8
  renovation grants 56–7
  rough sleeping 72
  rural housing 52
  Tenants' Charter 42
  Tenants' Choice 37, 47
  tenure 16
  Urban Investment Grant 65
  Urban Programme 64
Welsh Federation of Housing
  Associations 47
Welsh House Condition Survey 12
Welsh Office 60, 73

Printed in the UK for HMSO.
Dd.0296511, 3/93, C30, 51-2423, 5673.